KANSAS CITY CHIEFS

BY MARV ALINAS

The Child's World
childsworld.com

Published by The Child's World®
800-599-READ • childsworld.com

Photography Credits
© Andrew Mather/Kansas City Chiefs/AP Photo: 12–13; ChrisFloresFoto/Envato: football texture; Colin E. Braley/AP Photo: 19; Cooper Neill/AP Photo: cover, 2; David Gray/Kansas City Chiefs/AP Photo: 21; David Zalubowski/AP Photo: 17; G. Newman Lowrance/AP Photo: 11; Joe Robbins/AP Photo: 7; Kyle Rivas/Kansas City Chiefs/AP Photo: 15; oasisamuel/Shutterstock.com: 6, 9, (football); Ryan Kang/AP Photo: 4–5

ISBN Information
9781503875166 (Reinforced Library Binding)
9781503875456 (Portable Document Format)
9781503876491 (Online Multi-user eBook)
9781503877535 (Electronic Publication)

LCCN
2024952254

ABOUT THE AUTHOR

Marv Alinas has written dozens of books for children. When she's not reading or writing, Marv enjoys spending time with her family and traveling to interesting places. Marv lives in Minnesota.

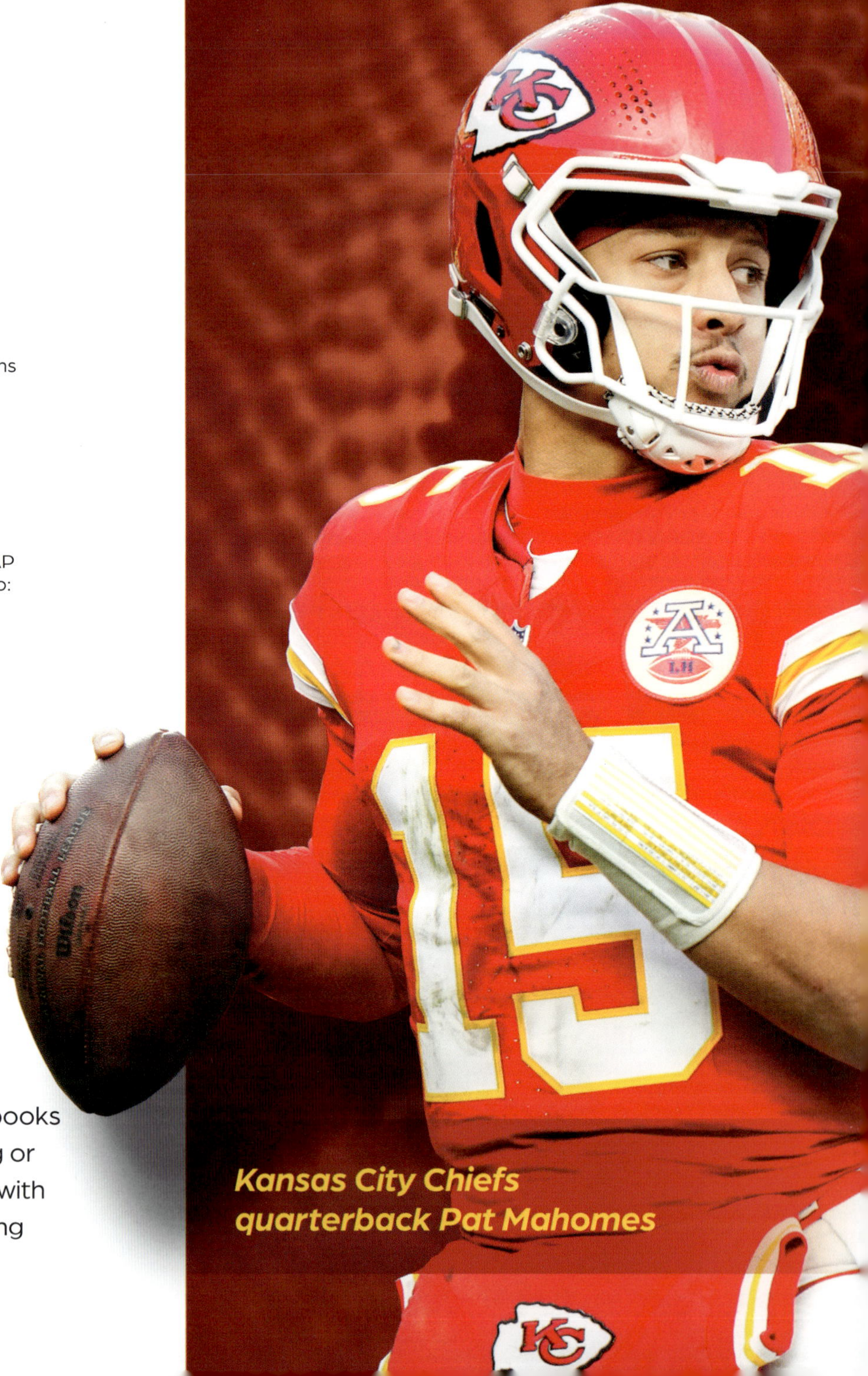

Kansas City Chiefs quarterback Pat Mahomes

CONTENTS

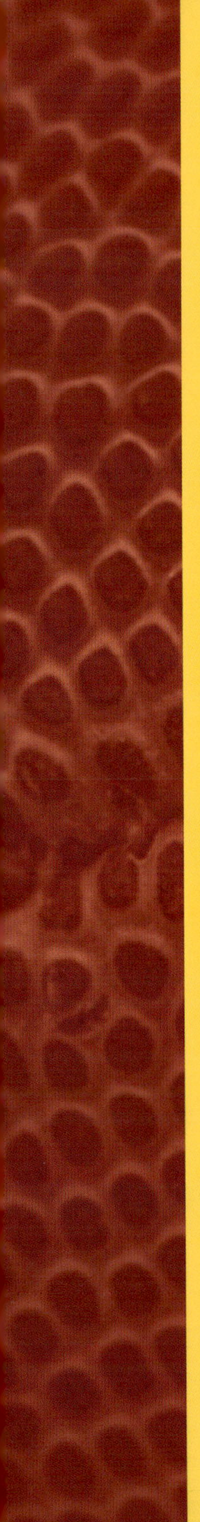

The Team

The Kansas City Chiefs are a football team. They play in Kansas City, Missouri. They started in 1959.

The Kansas City Chiefs run onto the field to play football.

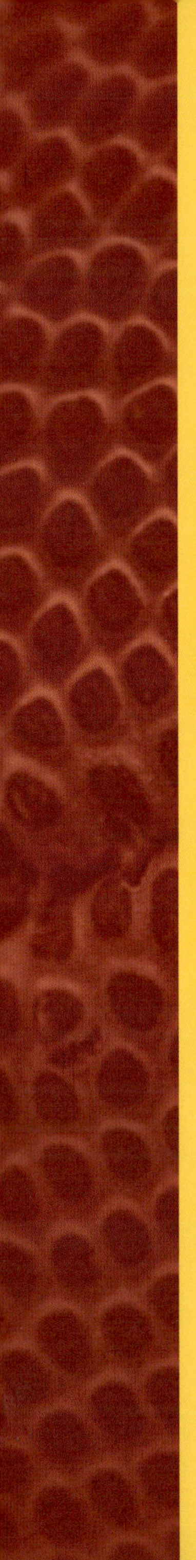

The Colors

Their team colors are red, gold, and white. Their **mascot** is a wolf. His name is KC Wolf.

The Chiefs used to have a live horse as their mascot. His name was Warpaint.

KC Wolf first appeared in 1989.

The Conference

The Chiefs are in the AFC West. The AFC stands for American Football **Conference**. There are three other teams in the AFC West.

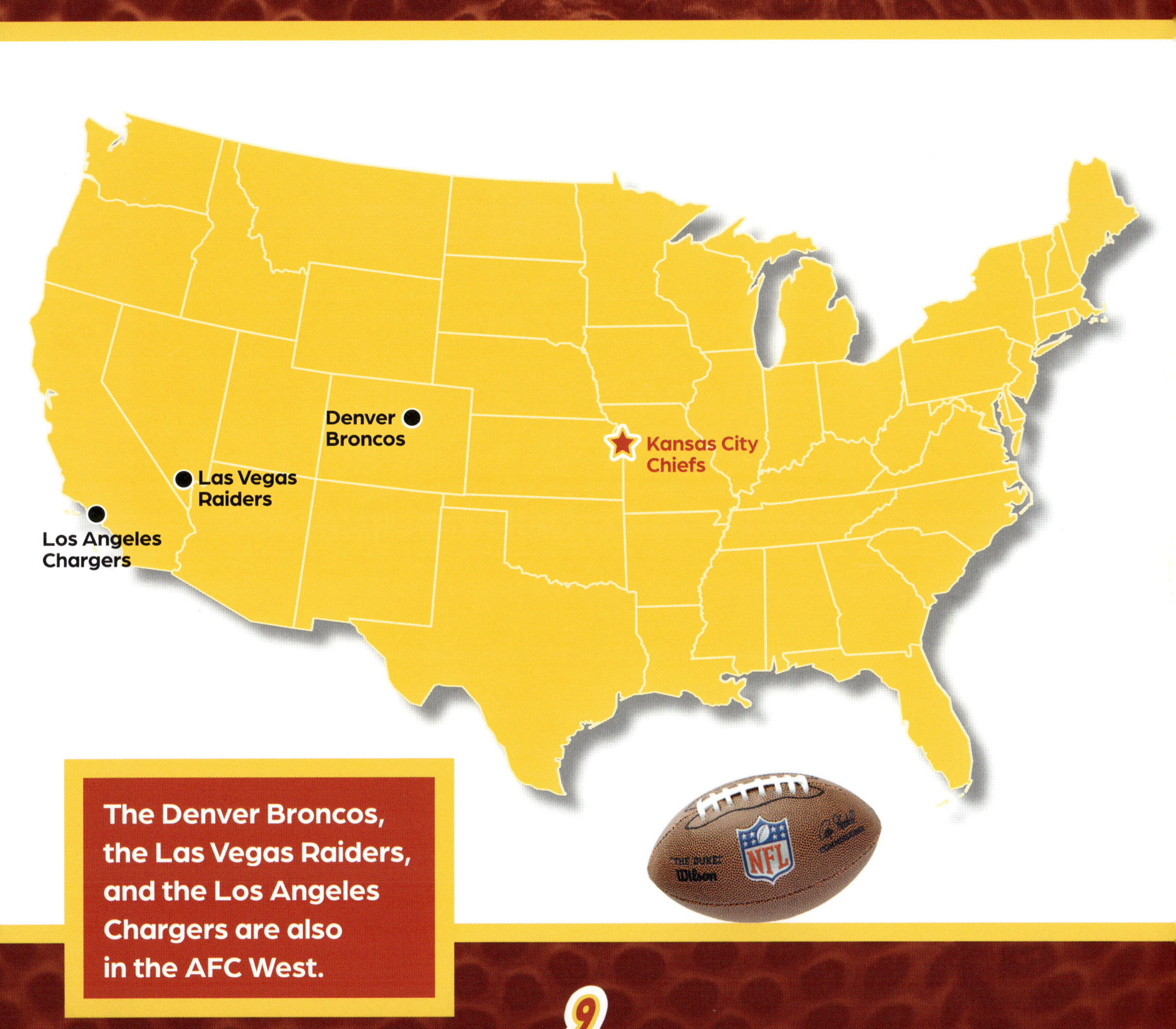

The Denver Broncos, the Las Vegas Raiders, and the Los Angeles Chargers are also in the AFC West.

The Stadium

The Chiefs play at Arrowhead **Stadium**. It opened in 1972. It can hold more than 76,000 people.

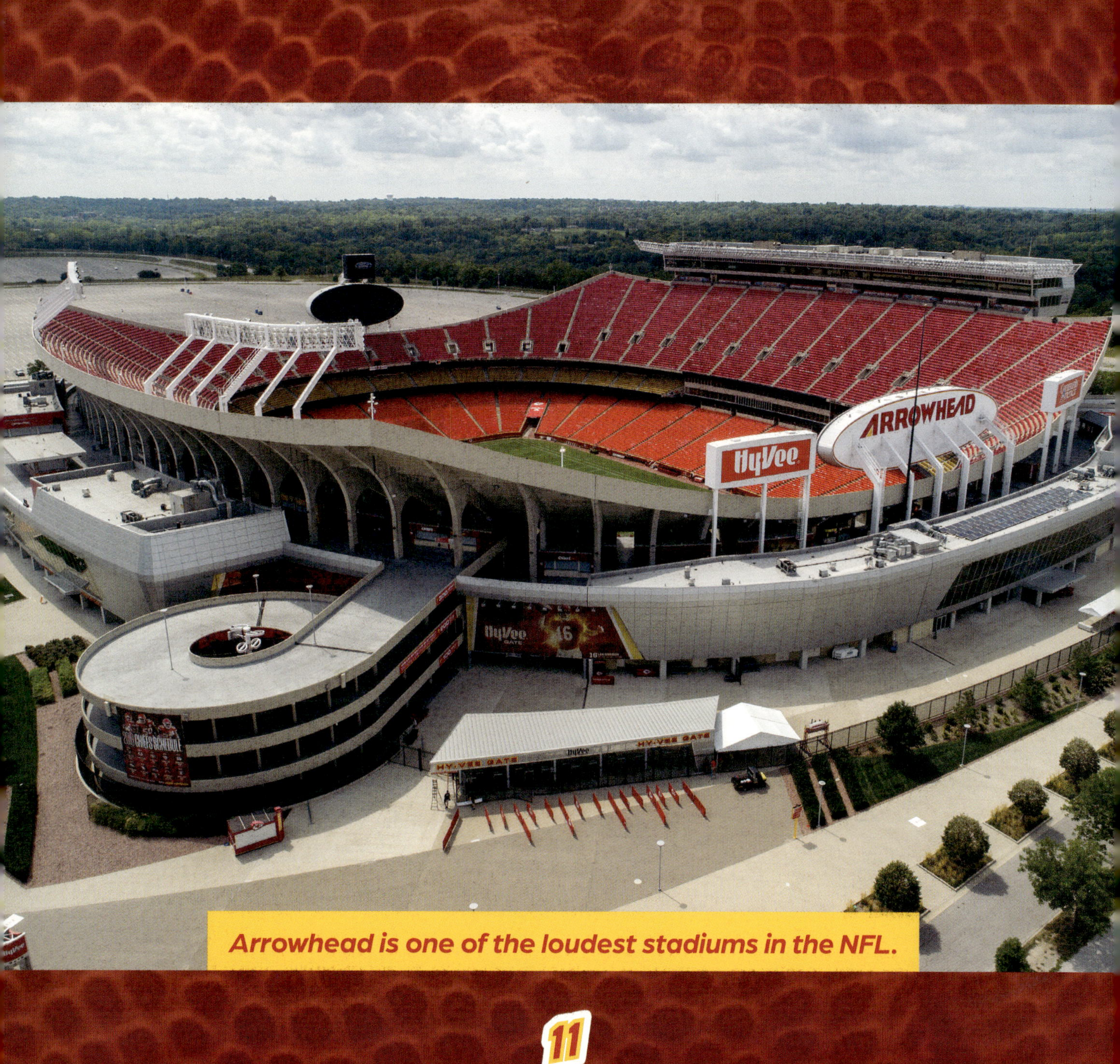

Arrowhead is one of the loudest stadiums in the NFL.

The Football Field

Yard lines
One yard hash marks
Goal post
End zone

Fun Fans

Fans of the Chiefs love to wear the team's colors. They call themselves the "Chiefs Kingdom." Many people wear a **jersey** with the number of their favorite player.

KC
KC

The Coaches

The Kansas City Chiefs have had 13 head coaches since they began. Andy Reid is the current coach. He has been the head coach since 2013.

Before coming to the Chiefs, Andy Reid coached the Philadelphia Eagles.

The Players

Many great players have been part of the Kansas City Chiefs. Some past greats include Tony Gonzalez and Derrick Thomas.

Current Chiefs stars are Patrick Mahomes, Travis Kelce, and Isiah Pacheco.

Patrick Mahomes and Travis Kelce celebrate after a great play.

They are exciting to watch during games.

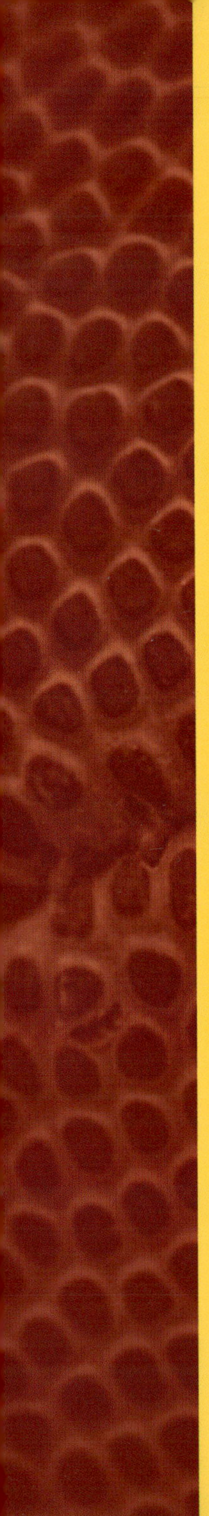

The Future

The Chiefs have gone to the **Super Bowl** seven times. They have won four times. They will keep trying for another win!

The Chiefs last won the Super Bowl in 2024.

FAST FACTS

- The Kansas City Chiefs play in Kansas City, Missouri.
- The team is in the AFC West.
- Arrowhead Stadium can hold more than 76,000 people.
- The Kansas City Chiefs have won the Super Bowl four times.

GLOSSARY

conference (KON–fur–enss): In sports, a conference is a grouping of teams.

jersey (JUR–zee): A jersey is a shirt sports players wear.

mascot (MAS–kot): In sports, a mascot is an animal, person, or thing that represents a team.

stadium (STAY–dee–um): A stadium is a large building where sports and concerts are held.

Super Bowl (SOO–pur BOWL): The Super Bowl is the championship game of the NFL.

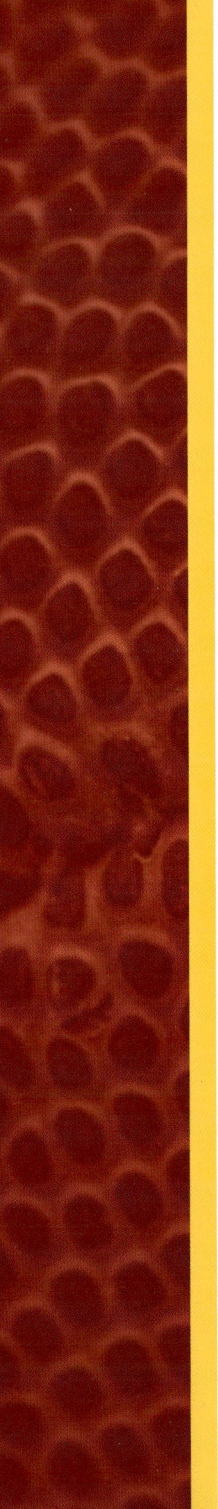

FIND OUT MORE

In the Library

Anderson, Josh. *Kansas City Chiefs.* Parker, CO: The Child's World, 2023.

Mattern, Joanne. *The Kansas City Chiefs.* Minneapolis, MN: Bellwether Media, 2024.

Whiting, Jim. *The Story of the Kansas City Chiefs.* Mankato, MN: Creative Education, 2025.

On the Web

Visit our website for links about the Kansas City Chiefs:
childsworld.com/links

Note to Parents, Caregivers, Teachers, and Librarians: We routinely verify our web links to make sure they are safe and active sites. So encourage your readers to check them out!

INDEX